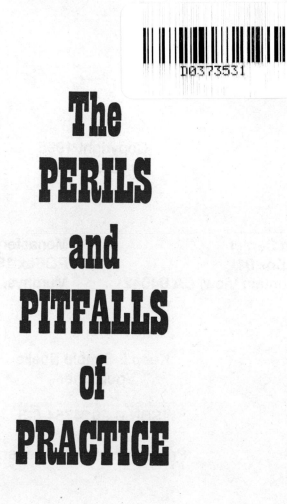

The
PERILS
and
PITFALLS
of
PRACTICE

Zen Center
POBox 91
Mountain View, CA 94042

Monastery/Retreat Center
POBox 1994
Murphys, CA 95247

Keep It Simple Books
-publisher-

ISBN 0-9614754-5-5

Printed on recycled paper.

ACKNOWLEDGMENTS

I would like to thank:

• All of us who have sat still long enough to have these questions.

• For technical assitance and expertise: Angelo, Ann, Cameron, Christa, Jeannie, Tricia.

• June Shiver — without whom these books could not exist.

Companion to
The Perils and Pitfalls of Practice

AUDIOTAPE

GETTING STARTED, GOING DEEPER
A Guide to Meditation

Instruction and guided meditation by Cheri Huber

Information: Who's Here? Productions, POBox 91, Mountain View, CA 94042

ISBN 0-9644401-0-5
Copyright 1994

WHOLESALE AVAILABLE

CONTENTS

iii

INTRODUCTION

What if you could look at your life with no belief that there's anything wrong with you or the world or anything else? If you were standing outdoors and the elements were beating on you, you wouldn't wonder why this was happening. You would know it was just weather. You would go inside. When you are miserable, suffering, trying to control things and it's just not working, you don't need to wonder why this is happening to you. It's just your conditioning. Go to center. At this point you might well ask, "But how can I do that?" I would have to respond that that's one of those trick questions because "I" can't do that.

About twenty questions into this project, I realized that the fundamental question of meditation practice (and of life) is this: am I at center and connected with my heart (wholeness, true nature, all that is, whole mind, essential self), or am I not at center and identified with egocentricity ("I", separate self, small mind, conditioning)? One of the primary reasons we practice awareness is to find out who's talking. Am I listening to the voice of my heart or the voice of egocentricity? It is clear that many of the questions posed to me about meditation are being asked by egocentricity, and it is important to realize that egocentricity does not want to meditate. Meditation brings us into the present and the egocentric, conditioned self doesn't exist in the present.

To have an experience of what we're talking about, take a long, deep breath and focus all of your attention on the breath. Now, look to see if while you're breathing, with all your attention focused on the breath, are there any problems? Any concerns? Fears, anxieties, upsets? Right then, while you're focusing. And I mean right before the voices start yelling at you saying, "This is stupid, focusing on your breath doesn't change anything. Just because you're not looking at them doesn't mean the problems have gone away. This isn't freedom, it's denial, avoidance..." Right before the conditioning kicks in, are there any problems?

It's not that there aren't situations and issues to be dealt with in life, but what would they look like without the hysteria of egocentricity, without the life-and-death-ness of the "I"? What would it be like to consider those issues without a voice warning you not to make mistakes, without dragging in the past or projecting failure in the future?

When you're focusing on the breath, when you're fully present and aware and attending right here and now, you have a chance to experience what it's like to live without the burden of conditioning.

In loving kindness,
Cheri

This book is offered

in loving kindness.

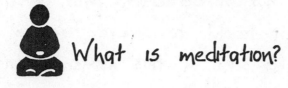 # What is meditation?

Before we explore this first
question, I want to explain some "rules of
the game." For instance, I don't have the
answers. Supposedly (and we must always
say "supposedly" under these circumstances
since obviously nobody knows for sure),
whenever anyone came to inquire of the
Buddha concerning these matters he would
respond with an encouragement to believe
nothing that he said. To this I have added:
Believe nothing that you say. The reason
for this is that believing keeps us from
being open to what is in this moment. So,
we attempt to believe nothing in order to
remain open and present to whatever we
are experiencing in this moment. When we
look closely we often find that our

experience is not in agreement with what we have been taught to believe. Freedom lies in being present in this moment. Clinging to conditioning, to beliefs, prevents us from being present, prevents us from being free.

There are many responses to every question. All I will offer you is my experience of Zen practice. You may then explore those experiences for yourself. Or not. No one can tell you what is true for you. Any teacher can only point the way. Each of us must make the journey for ourselves.

My constant responses to questions will include: I don't know; pay attention; believe nothing; and look to see. With that in mind we will explore together some common questions and concerns that I suspect most meditators have regardless of their chosen type of meditation.

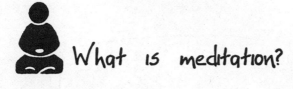# What is meditation?

For us, meditation is the practice of being aware, of paying attention in each moment to all that arises. It is an awareness/attention practice. We pay attention moment by moment in order to be in <u>this</u> <u>moment</u> rather than being drawn into the past or future by our conditioning. We attempt to be here, present, in this moment, now, with whatever is in this moment.

There have been occasions when I would refer to meditating while driving and people would become quite alarmed. They apparently had a picture of someone in a trance-like state behind the wheel of a car.

This is not my experience of
meditation. When I'm driving (walking, eating,
working, playing, thinking, sitting, resting, etc.),
I want to be fully present, awake, doing
what I'm doing and only what I'm doing.

It makes me a little nervous to
consider that everyone isn't meditating while
they're driving!

How can I know which type of meditation is right for me?

The difficulty with that question is that the "me" who is asking the question _is_ the difficulty. Because "me" (egocentricity, identity, the illusion of a separate self, self-image) will never find a meditation practice that is right for it. The reason is that meditation practice/awareness practice/paying attention is designed to take us beyond the illusion of an "I" or "me" that would be able to know such a thing. The one who wants to know is a conditioned process that is maintained through a failure to explore and examine beliefs and assumptions and opinions. Simply stated, I don't know who or what "I" is. How could I possibly know what's right for "me"? Those are the issues an awareness practice brings

5

to conscious awareness: Who am I? How do I know that? What makes me believe the things I believe? How do I know they're true? Who said so? What if they're not true?

I have heard that meditation reduces stress. Will Zen meditation do this for me?

No and yes. People will often ask me to teach them to meditate in order to relieve stress or to relax. I encourage them to pursue a different type of meditation, one that offers relaxation or stress reduction as its goals. So, no, these are not goals of Zen meditation.

To want to end stress and create a state of relaxation actually causes its own stress—between the experience that exists and the one we imagine would be better. In Zen practice, rather than trying to reduce or avoid stress, we allow ourselves to be with and fully experience the stress and tension. We ask: what are the sensations that I am labeling as stress?

how and where do I experience the sensations? do I suffer because of the sensations, or do I suffer because of what my mind tells me about the sensations and the meaning it ascribes to them? what conditioned beliefs do I have about the sensations?

As I pay attention to my experiences of stress, I become familiar with how stress operates and how I respond to it. In this process I develop a relationship to stress and might therefore be less a victim to it.

And, so, yes, the result might be that I am a less stressful person because I am less stressed about stress.

For many people the process of getting through the causes of tension and relaxation proves more of a challenge than they want to undertake. That's too bad. I think if people had fewer misconceptions about what a meditation practice is, they would be less discouraged when they find themselves having EXACTLY THE EXPERIENCE SITTING IS DESIGNED TO PRODUCE. We have not lived our lives in a calm, relaxed, peaceful way. When we sit down and sit still we're going to see that very clearly. That's good. If we were clear about what awareness practice is, our reaction would be YES!!! I'm really doing it! I'm having the paying attention experience! I'm seeing just how crazy I am!

I once met a monk who talked about his "rock'n'roll" mind. He spent all day in the monastery singing old rock'n'roll songs to himself. Many of us would think this was not correct monastic experience. His take on it was that he spent a lot of years teaching his mind to rock'n'roll, it might take a little while to un-teach it. He is a wise monk. It wasn't wrong to listen to rock'n'roll, it isn't wrong that it's still in his conditioning.

As he practices turning his attention away from the tunes and back to his breath, that conditioning will fade away.

This is practice. It is not a contest. There is no way to do it wrong. There is no right way to do it. We just pay attention, notice, drop it, and come back to the breath.

Some people meditate with eyes closed, some with eyes open. Which is best?

Awareness is best. Paying attention is best. Having said that, I will give you my best arguments for sitting with the eyes open. Most of us associate closing our eyes with going to sleep. Many people reach the state of deep relaxation that is available through sitting only when they are about to fall asleep. Closing the eyes while meditating is often an open invitation to sleep, and people have enough trouble staying awake in meditation even with their eyes open. People will often go into dream states or trance states when they're sleeping, and if they think they're meditating, think they're awake, they will believe the experiences they had while sleeping happened in an awake state. I remind folks that new religions can start this way, when someone believes the guidance and insights came from "on high" rather than from a nap.

Our practice is one of living in the mind of meditation always. If our sitting were with eyes closed, it would be very difficult to transition into daily life in the mind of meditation. For many of us our sight is our strongest sense. We are sitting still as a Buddha, and then, as soon as we open our eyes, we're back in the world of conditioning with only a waving relationship with our center, with the moment. So, if we accustom ourselves to sitting facing a blank wall (very helpful in narrowing the world down to just me, difficult to imagine that wall is doing anything to cause me to be the way I am) with our eyes just enough out of focus so that our sense of sight does not dominate, we can practice being present in a way that we can maintain when we stand up and reenter our daily life.

I can't clear my mind. What should I do?

Don't even try. Once again, the mind that wants to clear the mind is cluttering the mind. There's no reason to clear the mind. We don't know what the mind is, how it works, or who wants to clear it. There's so much fascinating stuff to experience between clutter mind and clear mind. Don't fall into the trap of thinking you want to take short cuts. Finding out who you are will be the most wonderful adventure you'll ever go on—don't miss any of it.

Sometimes I really want to meditate and sometimes I really don't want to. Any suggestions?

Odds are, if you stop to think about it, meditation isn't the first thing you've responded to in that way. That's how "small mind" (egocentricity, separate self, "I", etc.) responds to everything. The illusion of ourselves as separate beings is maintained in duality. That's why duality is so popular—it maintains egocentricity. Right and wrong, good and bad, this or that, us or them, for and against—anything that creates opposites. Opposition is the tension that keeps the delusion in place. That's one of the reasons this is often referred to as "the world of opposites." Heaven and hell, God and the devil, rich and poor, black and white, male and female. So, of course, you don't always

15

want to meditate. We don't always want to do anything. The <u>wanting</u> and <u>not wanting</u> shouldn't surprise us. That it continues to surprise us should surprise us.

In spite of all our experience to the contrary, we continue to believe that we will find something that will make us different. I will find a magic pill and suddenly everything will be different, I will be the way I want me to be all the time.

FOR THE PERFECT YOU
☆ ☆ MAGIC PILL ☽ ☆
TAKE ONE A DAY

All an awareness practice will do is help us see how silly most of the things we've been taught to believe really are. Just notice: ah, I'm really wanting to sit; ah, sitting is not being so much fun. Liking and disliking doesn't mean anything except I'm liking and disliking. It doesn't mean I should or should not do anything. I've decided to meditate and so I shall, even though on any given day I might like it and I might not.

We often talk about the toothbrushing approach to meditation. When we're young we battle brushing our teeth. I don't want to and why should I? Then we get older and dental appointments, cavities, social acceptance, and possibly dental bills help us know that we will, in fact, brush our teeth regularly whether we feel like it or not. When meditation reaches the same level of importance in our lives, we will sit, whether we feel like it or not.

I notice you usually say "sitting" instead of meditation. What's the difference?

There are so many types of meditation and so many understandings and misunderstandings about meditation that I find it helpful to use a word that doesn't carry a lot of associations for people. The word "sitting" has connotations that are quite in keeping with our practice.

I'm often asked, "Do you mean just <u>sitting</u> <u>there</u>? Aren't you <u>doing</u> anything?" The answer is yes, just sitting there, and no, not doing anything. Sitting is just sitting, being present, paying attention. No controlling, disciplining, clearing. Just being present and noticing all that arises.

My legs often fall asleep
when I sit. What causes
that?

There are many things that can
cause the legs to fall asleep. One of the
most common is wearing clothing that binds
behind the knees because it is too tight or
made of heavy fabric. It's good to wear
loose, soft clothing when you sit. A second
common cause is sitting too far back,
forward, or to the side of your cushion.
The buttocks should be placed on the
cushion so that the "sits" bones are on
the front third of the cushion. If there is
too much pressure on the back of the
upper thigh, the leg will often fall asleep.
Also, it is good to switch legs with each
sitting. Whether you are sitting in Burmese,
half-lotus, or full lotus, place the right foot

in front of or upon the left thigh in one sitting and then the left foot in front of or upon the right thigh in the next sitting. You might try making your cushion higher or lower by adding or removing kapok. If the difficulty persists, go to a Zen center and ask someone who is a seasoned sitter to check your posture. You might also try sitting in front of a mirror. Sometimes you can see misalignments that you can't feel.

How long should I meditate?

For the rest of your life! Sorry. It seems to me that we set standards and make up rules so that we can get out of things. We read somewhere about meditating an hour in the morning and an hour in the evening and decide that's what we should do and three days later meditation is a thing of the past. If you meditate five minutes a day, five days a week, it will change your life. There's a "because" with that which is: if you're drawn to meditation it's probably because on some level you know you need it. You want it. Your life isn't working the way you suspect it could and there's a lot of information that suggests sitting, being still, coming back to yourself could make a difference. So give yourself a chance to be successful. If you sit for five minutes a day for five days, the odds are very good that you're going to enjoy it and you'll want to do more. If that's so, then up it to ten minutes the next week. When ten is too few, up it to fifteen and so forth until you're sitting for thirty minutes at a time. We never sit for more than thirty minutes at a sitting, and if we want to sit more, we get up and do some walking meditation and then sit for another period.

See if you can avoid making sitting a "should." We put things on the should list when we don't want to do them. We always do what we truly want to do, so keep meditation on the want list. If you miss a day it doesn't mean you're a failure and will never sit again. Sit again the next day. It's not a bad thing to miss something. Instead of beating yourself up for not sitting, just notice how much you miss it when you don't have it.

One very strong encouragement: always keep agreements with yourself. If you've agreed to sit for five minutes, sit for five minutes—not for four and not for six. Establish a trust with yourself. If you're having a great time, when the five minutes is up, stand up and do a little walking meditation and then go back for another period.

I have a lot of back pain when I sit.

This is a broad issue and so I'll attempt to speak to the most common back pain questions. Sitting is like many other new activities in that not much of the rest of our lives prepares us for it. Many people don't have good posture. Many people have very weak muscles in their backs. Then the person who has poor posture and weak back muscles sits down with a group and tries to sit bolt upright for thirty minutes, nearly dies, and decides meditation is a big mistake.

Think of sitting as a sport. You have to train up. I always encourage people to learn to sit when they're not meditating. Practice sitting, standing, and walking with good posture. Sit cross-legged while watching

TV or reading. Start an exercise program to help strengthen your back. Be patient. If you wanted to start running, you wouldn't begin your running career with a marathon. Keep sitting, keep focusing on the posture, and over time the pain will go away. Yes, as inconceivable as it seems, most people who have been sitting for a good while sit without physical pain.

Is there a best time of day to meditate?

Over the years I've concluded that the best time to meditate is up to the individual. I'm not a morning person and have slept through an extraordinary number of early morning meditations. I know many people who find the wee hours of the morning to be the most perfect time to sit. I tend to enjoy most the sittings that transition me from work day to evening. And I've heard from many meditators that if they don't sit first thing in the morning they never seem to get to it. Once again, find out. See what is so for you, see what works best for you, and set your schedule accordingly.

Can kids learn to meditate?

It's been my experience that just about anybody can do just about anything they really want to do. I've never encouraged teaching children to meditate unless THEY really want to do it. And it seems to me that if children are around people who are paying attention, attending to themselves, aware of others, and living their lives in a compassionate manner, they will naturally be influenced and attracted. The irony is that kids don't need to learn to meditate—they live in the mind of meditation until we socialize them out of it. As in many situations, teaching children to meditate is probably less about what to do and more about what not to do.

My knees hurt a lot when I sit. Is there a "best" posture for bum knees?

Many years ago, after I was already committed to sitting, I injured my back very seriously. It was the kind of injury that I've watched cripple a lot people. Being crippled was simply not an option for me because sitting was far too important to have anything interfere with it. I dedicated my life to returning my back to a condition that could tolerate any amount of sitting I wanted to do. It took tremendous effort and attention and patience and was one of the finest learning experiences of my life. Since I have to constantly maintain that level of attention in order not to re-injure myself, I consider my back one of my greatest allies in practice. I am grateful each day for the back injury, for the healing, and for all it has taught me and continues to teach me.

Perhaps instead of seeing those knees as bum and assuming they aren't equal to the task, it might be interesting to find out what's possible.

I've tried to do a meditation practice dozens of times. I sit for a while and then I quit. How do I learn the self-discipline necessary to stick with it?

We observe often that people will come to spiritual practice when they've suffered enough. No amount of talking or wheedling or guilt or shoulds will convince somebody to do something as difficult as embracing the ego and ending suffering if they're not really ready. Perhaps you could think of all those starts and stops as "getting ready." Perhaps you could focus on all the sitting you've done rather than on the sitting you haven't done. And perhaps the most helpful thing you could do is to get fascinated by the process of starting and stopping. How does that happen? How does it work? Now that would be an interesting thing to know because I'll bet sitting is not the only thing you've started and stopped. It will take a well-developed ability to pay attention while you're seeing how that happens, and that's where meditation will come in handy.

I would love to meditate, but I can't imagine how I could do that with two little kids.

I can't imagine having two little kids and not meditating! We just published a book called Time-Out for Parents, which we hope will help parents figure out how they can meditate (be present) and parent at the same time.

I don't have much respect for setting hard-and-fast standards because it seems to me that we tend to use them as an excuse for not being present. And we often choose a standard over compassion, and I think choosing anything over compassion is not a good idea. Parenting, more than anything I can think of, requires us either to drop our standards, severely lower our standards, or, at the very least, recognize the suffering inherent in standards.

Parenting is a humbling experience, is it not? There are so many fictions we can simply no longer maintain. And if we can see our egos take a beating in this and have a chuckle over it, it can bring a great deal of sympathy for the human condition. But if the ego takes parenting as another opportunity to beat us up, then it is sad indeed because there is no increase in compassion, only in suffering. So, in support of lowering those standards that cause suffering, see if you can master the one minute meditation. See how many one minute meditation periods you can get in in a day. You'll be able to have them while attending someone on the potty chair, or waiting after your tenth request to "please put your socks on as I asked you," or any of the thousands of such moments that arise in each day. You can learn to bring your attention to your breath as a way of calming and centering. Little kids are in the present moment. You have a wonderful excuse to be in the present, too. You have to be there with them.

This is what you've got. This is your training and your practice. Perhaps you imagine that if you didn't have small children meditation would be a snap. Let me reassure you there would be some other insurmountable—there is for all of us until we get it that there is no parallel universe in which we're living the life we're SUPPOSED to be living.

This is it. There is no alternative. Once we see that we can stop agonizing and get on with the business of being present to exactly what is.

I can sit on a cushion just fine. What I can't do is pay attention.

How do you know you're not paying attention?

I really hope you will stop and consider that question seriously. How do you know you're not paying attention? If you weren't paying attention, how would you know you're not paying attention? Don't you need to be paying attention to what you are or are not attending to in order to make that determination? So you see, you are paying attention. Just because you're not paying attention to what you think you SHOULD be paying attention to doesn't mean you're not paying attention. If I've decided that I want to focus on the tip of my nose, but instead I'm focusing on my

big toe, it doesn't mean I'm not focusing.
It's very important not to confuse content
with process. Conditioned mind would like us
always to focus on content (the whats, the
"stuff" of life). When we focus on content,
conditioning can just pull us from thing to
thing to thing in such a way that we
never know what's happening to us. I'm so
busy worrying about my job, my kids, my
husband's health, my sister's marriage, etc.,
that I fail to notice that the constant,
the <u>process</u>, is "worry." When I see how I
do the <u>process</u> of worry, my relationship
with all that <u>content</u> changes immediately.
Instead of getting all caught up in, or
hopelessly bogged down in, BELIEVING every
situation, my reaction might be more, "Ah,
worry. I'm in the conditioned habit of
worrying." Then I can come to this
moment and simply be present with what is
right now.

What do I focus on when I'm sitting?

In our practice, we focus our attention on the breath. For me, that's an experience of bringing all my attention to the part of the body that is most immediately engaged in the act of breathing. I focus on the breath as it enters the body, fills the body, and leaves the body. Focusing as completely as possible; not pushing anything away. It's not a matter of tensing muscles or closing down. In fact, as we practice focusing the attention, there is an awareness that the attention moves within the field of awareness. So as I'm staying with the breath as it fills my body, as my abdomen expands, I am still aware of the parts of the body the breath has already moved through and the rest of the body as well. At the top of the breath, as the breath enters the body, there is an awareness of the lower abdomen expanding; and at the bottom of the breath, as the lower abdomen contracts and the air moves out, there is an awareness of the throat and the nostrils releasing the air.

Staying with the breath from entering the body to leaving the body. This is sometimes referred to as following the breath. A technique that's often used to assist in this process is counting the breath. One takes a breath in and with the exhalation silently counts "one." With the next exhalation, "two," and so on until ten. If the mind wanders off, one is encouraged to patiently and compassionately bring the mind back from whence it has wandered and begin counting at one. This is not to make a contest. We are simply not practiced at being present, and without a reference point, we can wander for a long time. Sometimes the counting is simple and effortless. Sometimes we "come to" at 13 or 46. Sometimes we can't get to 4. Just notice. Just sit still and pay attention. Not trying to accomplish anything; holding on to nothing; pushing nothing away; allowing everything to be exactly as it is.

People sometimes fall into the habit of believing they're qualified to distinguish a "good" meditation from a "bad" meditation. Not a helpful habit. Every meditation is a good meditation. Someone said to me recently, "All we have to do is show up and accept the miracles." So true. And it's good to remember that miracles are sometimes difficult to recognize in the moment in which they are happening.

Aren't there a lot of meditation techniques? How do I know which one to use?

Most traditions have their own approach to meditation. Here are a couple of ideas I offer to people who ask the "which one?" question.

Spiritual practice is like a relationship. We fall in love and then find out that loving is harder than falling. We get to the point of realizing that we're stuck with a regular old human being instead of the god or goddess we thought we were getting, and we sometimes want to rethink our decision. At this point it can be helpful to remind ourselves: this is what I wanted. I wanted to love and be loved. This is a good, decent, human, human being. This is what it means to be a human loving a human. It's not easy and it's worth it. I'm probably not going to find anyone any better (over the long haul) so I might as well be where I am and do what I'm doing.

The same is true with meditation. If you were attracted in the beginning, stick with it because if you begin to let conditioned mind decide you should quit when it gets uncomfortable, it will be a quick trip down hill. Egocentricity (conditioning, small mind, identity, illusion of separateness) is NEVER going to like meditation because meditation is going to remove the illusion of the solidity of egocentricity itself.

Imagine that you are going to dig for water. You take your shovel, pick a spot, and take three or four scoops of dirt and no water. So you move over a few feet and repeat the process. No water. You try again a few feet away—

nothing. With this method you could cover the land masses of the earth and not find water. Or you could pick a spot that looks good, feels right, others have said will work, and you just start digging and you don't stop, no matter what (regardless of content or "stuff") until you hit water.

So pick a practice you're attracted to, one with a good reputation, start, and don't quit.

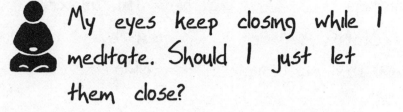 My eyes keep closing while I meditate. Should I just let them close?

Keeping the eyes open during sitting is difficult for many folks at first. It often happens that when we attempt something unfamiliar, we feel awkward and unskilled. Mostly it's just a big struggle until we have practiced enough to begin to feel comfortable. Usually we don't even know when the transition happens. Perhaps one day someone says something that reveals their discomfort and you remember that you used to feel that way. So, when your eyes close, savor that delicious relief for a moment and then open them again.

Your attention is not meant to be in the eyes when you're sitting. You're not looking. You could see, but you're not looking. This way you begin to associate meditation practice with open eyes and you'll minimize your chances of falling asleep.

I've heard you talk about not wearing jeans when we sit. Why? Are there other "dos and don'ts"?

I don't see "dos and don'ts" with practice, I see "helps and hindrances." It certainly is not the case that we <u>shouldn't</u> wear jeans or that we're not <u>supposed</u> to wear jeans, although you might find a group with whom you would like to sit who does have a "respectful dress code." The reason I discourage jeans is that they, like other thick or tight clothing, can restrict circulation and lead to your legs falling asleep. So it isn't a big moral issue or anything.

Other "helps and hindrances" that are often confused with "dos and don'ts" are: avoiding eye contact; minimizing reading and journal writing; being silent more often.

These practices are usually emphasized when on retreat and practicing with a group and can be quite helpful additions to the everyday life of a person wishing to be more present and aware.

Now I would like to say a few words about the benefits of following guidelines in an awareness practice. We're very well conditioned by adulthood to believe that there's a right and wrong way to do everything. The conditioned mind believes it knows exactly how everything <u>should</u> be. A huge part of practice is seeing that belief system and seeing through it. But how are we going to see it if we're caught up in it and in fact seeing <u>through</u> it as if it were a pair of glasses? A quick way to see our conditioning is to face situations in which we are encouraged <u>not to act out of it</u>. So we have guidelines.

There are certain conditioned behaviors that are fairly well known as sources of suffering. A simple example is that many of us have been taught to believe that we need to be "nice" and that if we are nice to others, whatever that means in any given situation, then people will (should, ought to, are obligated to, will want to) be nice to us in return. So I go for a retreat at the Interfaith Retreat Center and discover there are guidelines to be silent and not make eye contact with others. I may not be aware of the strength of my conditioning to be nice until getting into this situation where guidelines prevent me from doing these little social niceties like looking at someone and smiling, or chatting with someone during a meal. The guideline has prevented me from mindlessly acting out of my conditioning. Now it's right there for me to see in the

47

form of an urgent desire to talk to someone, to interact in some way that establishes that I am nice and people like me. By discouraging habitual acting out of conditioning, the guidelines enable me to see and feel how driven I am by that conditioning.

Another example is sitting itself. In our practice we face a blank white wall for thirty minutes when we're sitting together as a group. It is understood that people are still and quiet and remain seated for the whole time. Just <u>that</u> is enough to set off conditioned mind, and if one is paying attention one can see one's whole life pass by in the ensuing battle. The guideline to sit still and quiet for thirty minutes will unleash an amazing creativity from egocentricity of the most convincing reasons for getting up and leaving the room. Coughing and choking attacks are very popular, and remembering something important that needs to be done immediately (did I remember to turn off the stove?) can be quite effective. If I can learn to be free when conditioned mind is threatening me with everything from vomiting to fainting to death if I don't stop sitting, I can be free anywhere, any time.

Will I be controlled by conditioning or free? Following guidelines is sometimes the only way we can find the courage _not_ to do what our conditioning tells us to do.

I know we're encouraged not to move during meditation. That feels cruel to me.

I know. All I can do is encourage you to consider that the one who sees it as cruel wants you to stop meditating so it can remain in control. In other words, egocentricity wants to make sure that it, not some "outside authority," is in charge of telling you what to do.

It's good to remember that the reason most of us begin meditating is that our small, conditioned mind and its programmed voices are driving us mad. Figuratively if not literally. So the same voice that tells you you are lazy, undisciplined, and a hopeless failure will say it's cruel to learn to sit still when you want to move. If you learn to see through the process of urgency that is the cornerstone of conditioned mind, if you realize that it is perfectly possible, even easy, to sit still regardless of thoughts in your mind, what will those voices have to threaten you with, to control you with?

It is extremely important to see that in this issue there is not just one "you." You are dealing with the part of you who wants peace, clarity, joy, and well-being, the part who wants you to meditate; and the part of you who is frightened, surviving, driven by the past and the future, the socialized, conditioned self, the part of you who does <u>not</u> want you to meditate. Keep in mind that egocentricity (conditioned mind) will always see efforts to remove its control as cruel and unfair.

Sometimes it feels like the voices are going to drive me crazy. Is that a danger?

This question always makes me chuckle because it's such a perfect dramatization of where we all find ourselves regularly with an awareness practice. Supposedly (here's that "supposedly" again), the Buddha at one time stated "Society is insane." Twenty five hundred years ago he noticed that. We're all "crazy." That's what socialization does to us. In fact, it often seems to me that some of the folks society labels as crazy are simply failing to go along with the program society has decided is sane. Do we really need to look farther than the magazine racks at our local supermarket check-out stand to know that the Buddha was accurate?

So what happens to a lot of us is that we sit down and start paying attention and we become _more_ _aware_ of just how crazy we are! And it scares us because we don't know it's been going on until we notice it. But it has been going on. We can just check with someone who loves us, and they will share with us (we hope in a gentle, loving, compassionate way) that, indeed, we've been pretty crazy all along. We start from a place of inherent adequacy and we are socialized into fearful, neurotic, anxious, insecure "adults." Then we fit in.

In Buddhism we even have a phrase for this specific experience. It's called "going farther and faring worse." As we become more subtly aware, we become more aware of subtleties. So we see ourselves more clearly and we're horrified by what we see. This is where we have to face hard questions like, "Do I want to be free or do I want to keep up my self-image? Do I want to be right or do I want to end suffering?" If we want to be free, if we want to end suffering, we're going to have to see through and let go all the conditioned beliefs we've assumed and believed were who we are. They are not who you are; they are brain-washing, programming, conditioning. When you sit down and watch your small, conditioned mind in action, you will see a great deal about <u>what</u> <u>happened</u> to you, but you probably won't see a whole lot about who you truly are.

What do you mean by egocentricity?

We use the term egocentricity to point toward that conditioned belief in a separate identity that we call "I." It's not true that we are separate, it just <u>appears</u> that way. It's an illusion. It's an illusion in the same way that it's an illusion that the magician makes the elephant disappear from the stage. Because we don't see what happened, it <u>seems</u> like the elephant vanished into thin air. And for us it <u>seems</u> like we are separate. This illusion causes us to see ourselves as the center of the universe, not as a reference point or a perspective, but actually as the most important thing. As we see through this appearance, as we experience the non-separateness of all existence, our frantic focus on <u>my</u>, <u>me</u> and mine begins to fall away. We don't have to get rid of it, it just falls away when we see it for the fiction that it is. That's one of the big reasons we don't encourage people to try to change. The trying and the changing are tools egocentricity uses to stay stuck. Believing that something is wrong perpetuates the belief that it is real. It is not real. It's an illusion. For instance, when I decide I'm selfish (and that's wrong), I decide I should try to change that about myself. Einstein once stated that it's not possible to solve a problem with the same mind that created it. For us that means that the same small, conditioned, limited mind that believes "selfish" is a true and real condition is now going to end that condition. You can see the inherent difficulties! But, when we realize (see, know, and understand experientially) what this illusory state called "selfish" is; when we see through our

56

conditioned beliefs and let go of our assumption that we are the center of the actual universe and that each thing we do or don't do is going to make the difference for the world; when we no longer have the need to judge or hate ourselves; then the whole issue will simply fall away. We see ourselves as an integral, essential part of all that is, and we no longer need to live in the duality of: I must have everything/I can't have anything. We realize that we're enough, and there's enough, and there is nothing wrong. There's no problem with anything. Every event, every moment in life is our best opportunity to see how we cause ourselves to suffer, to let that go, to be present and end suffering.

Is it OK to swallow, cough, sneeze, belch, scratch, etc., during meditation?

I think the original question was about coughing and I added the others because I get questions about each of them as well. The encouragement (the _strong_ encouragement) is not to indulge any such practices. And they _are_ "practices." There's a habit I failed to mention, clearing the throat, that sometimes reaches epidemic proportions in our Sangha. We have an epidemic because we're so accustomed to clearing the throat that we don't even hear it. The person who is making the sound doesn't hear it; to others it can seem as if the "sound of one throat clearing" is the root sound of the universe If I can make a constant sound of clearing my throat and not notice it, what other mindless habits am I engaged in? And what would it take to bring that one habit to the front of my conscious awareness so that I no longer mindlessly perpetuate it? This is the point.

A great deal of suffering occurs because we believe that if we _feel_ something we have to _do_ something. Not so. When I realize that I can itch and not scratch, the application of that principle is limitless. What does an itch feel like? Where does it begin? On the skin? In the mind? How big is it? Does it move? How long does it last left to itself? What happens when I focus all my attention on it? What happens when I turn my attention away? Now, I'm not suggesting you ask and answer all those questions. I'm pointing to an attitude of mind. If you were present and paying attention you would know the answers to those questions and more. You would be sitting there seeing with an uncluttered, unlimited awareness, and there would be clarity.

So, no. Don't move. Don't believe sneezes just happen. Don't believe coughing or scratching or belching or any other human experiences are just things to be victimized by. Find out what is going on.

When we practice together as a group, we are creating a privileged environment. As we all attend to ourselves, as we turn the attention inward, as we take responsibility for our own experience (responsibility, not fault or blame), we create together, for ourselves and one another, a three-dimensional version of the blank white wall we face in formal sitting. It's a safe place for me to experience "me" and the conditioning that results in my suffering.

When I can't sleep at night is it good to meditate, or should I just lie there and watch the parade of chattering characters go by?

It is always good to pay attention. We don't encourage people to lie down when they meditate because it's like inviting sleep and we don't want to associate sleep with meditation.

There is an expression in Buddhism: with the ideal comes the actual. I can't sleep. Should I pay attention? Should I come back to the present or simply follow the conditioning in and out of hell states? I, personally, would go with the paying attention.

There are three "types" of awareness that we begin to notice in practice. The first is simple lack of awareness or consciousness. I'm going around in the world and even though it sort of seems like I'm aware, I kind of know what's going on, I could tell you what town I'm in and who I'm with, I'm not <u>present</u>.

The second is the place in which I've learned to see, primarily, <u>what</u> I'm doing. When I see it, my conditioning tells me I shouldn't be behaving that way and I try to stop. So awareness becomes associated with punishment and feeling bad. Again, I'm not any different, I'm just aware of how I'm being, and the discomfort is so great I'd rather go back to being that way and not knowing it.

In the third "type," I can learn to stop taking my conditioning personally, I can see that how I'm behaving is the result of <u>what happened to me</u> rather than <u>who I am</u>, and I can be grateful for the awareness that will lead me to freedom. I will learn to say "thank you" each time I see myself, regardless of what I see, and this is the stage of real spiritual growth. Now the _how_ of how I cause myself to suffer is available to me—I can see it, accept it, embrace it, and let go. Freedom.

How do I know when I'm in the moment? What does it feel like?

The difficulty with this question is that we are trying to talk about something that cannot be talked about. There is an image in Zen, a finger pointing at the moon. It's very easy for us to get caught up looking at the finger and not notice where it's pointing. Anything I would say concerning what it feels like to be in the present moment would be a finger pointing at the moon because I can't <u>say</u> what it feels like.

Thoughts and speech are metaphorical. All we can do is talk about what something is like. Talking about it happens after the fact, from somewhere outside it. We can say, "I'm having such-and-such an experience." No. By the time I say I'm having it, I'm no longer having it. It's now a memory that I'm talking about, a very recent one perhaps, but a memory nonetheless.

How does it feel? I can only point: It's a feeling of belonging, of well-being, of all-rightness. It's a lack of tension, stress, and worry. There is comfort and ease and peace.

If I'm having these experiences, I might be tempted to wonder if I am in the present moment. As soon as I begin wondering about the experience, I am no longer in the experience. I have left it in order to think or talk about it. If I try to possess it, grasp it and make it mine, I lose it. This is because being in the present moment is not a process of grasping and holding on but of releasing and letting go.

How can you meditate when you have no time to meditate?

The old line about that is, "If you're too busy to meditate, you're too busy." Only egocentricity, only the illusion of separateness, is "too busy." The present moment is absolutely spacious. In the moment there is always room (and time) for the moment. Only when we feel separate and we're trying to live in the past or the future (the domains of egocentricity); only when we're trying to do what is not ours to do at a time that is not the time to do it are we "too busy." Too busy keeps egocentricity at the center of the universe, in the pivotal position, and keeps us in its control. Egocentricity says, "IF YOU DON'T LISTEN TO ME AND DO EVERYTHING

I TELL YOU TO DO EXACTLY WHEN AND HOW I TELL YOU TO DO IT SOMETHING AWFUL WILL HAPPEN TO YOU!

If I believe this threat, something awful is already happening to me. Instead of living life in the joy and comfort and peace that is my birthright, I am living my life in the fear and anxiety and pressure that I've been conditioned to believe is who I am. The suffering of life exists because of our beliefs, not because of life. It is my experience that egocentricity, fear, suffering, the illusion of a separate identity, and "I" are synonymous terms.

You stress physical posture in meditation. Does that mean that a person who is physically incapable of getting into meditation posture can't meditate?

Absolutely not. In fact there's a wonderful story told in Phillip Kapleau's <u>Three</u> <u>Pillars</u> <u>of</u> <u>Zen</u> about a young Japanese women who had one of the most profound enlightenment experiences of recent times while bedridden and dying. It's just that it's so much easier in proper sitting posture.

The best thing I can liken it to is taking up a sport. If you were going to play golf, I suppose that in the beginning it wouldn't matter much if you held the club like a baseball bat, you're probably not going to hit the ball anyway. But as you get more involved with the game, hitting the ball will become more important—it is, after all, a big part of the game. So form is going to become an increasing focus. You begin to realize that if you hold the club, address the ball, and swing correctly, you're going to increase immeasurably your odds of hitting that ball. In fact, you begin to realize that all this mental agony from, "This feels so awkward," to "I don't think it works for me to keep that arm straight," to "I'm going to miss it!" is not helpful, it's the difficulty. Exactly the same in sitting. If you want to sit, learn to sit properly. See if you can be willing to trust that centuries of practice have rendered an understanding of an excellent way to place the body in order to aid the harmonizing of body and mind. Once you learn to do it, the posture is comfortable, relaxing, supportive of attention and awareness, and easily maintained for extended periods of time. Worth pursuing IF YOU WANT TO MEDITATE. So, as with everything, check to see if the heart does and the ego doesn't, or vice versa. If from your heart you sense meditation is for you, then make the effort and learn to see through and not believe the voices that say, "It's too hard; I'm bored; I don't want to; I don't like this."

What is meditation going to do for me when I only have weeks to live?

What will _not_ meditating do for you when you only have weeks to live? Remember that meditation as we define it is paying attention, being present, being aware and with yourself, being here in this moment. If I knew death was near, I wouldn't want to miss a second of my life. Remember, fear can exist only when we're _not_ in the moment. Fear cannot exist without beliefs, and in the moment there is nothing to believe, there is only what is. It seems to me that the "me" who believes itself to be separate, who was "born" and now fears that it will "die" would be greatly comforted by the refuge of the present.

How can I meditate when I'm in so much pain?

Again, how can one not? In our practice we differentiate pain from suffering. It seems that pain in life is inevitable. We suffer when we try to avoid the inevitable, the pain of life. In this light we can say "Suffering is optional."

I don't see where meditation is getting me. I don't feel any different.

I'm going to keep emphasizing this point: the one who makes those statements is the difficulty. Only egocentricity looks at life in terms of "What is in this for me? If I don't see a reward for me right away, I'm not interested." So the "I" who can't see that it's getting anywhere and doesn't feel any different, won't. Egocentricity trying to understand whole mind (true nature, inherent adequacy, wholeness, nonseparateness, etc.) is like your toaster trying to understand electricity. It's a fish trying to comprehend the ocean. It's not possible, and we would save ourselves a lot of suffering if we understood that. "Well, what about... Well, I don't understand why...

Well, it doesn't make sense to me that..."
That's right, it doesn't and it won't. Don't
confuse yourself. The fact that small mind
can't grasp something doesn't mean the
something isn't so, it just means small mind
can't grasp it. Small mind grasps very little
outside its own conditioning, and it can't
even see that.

　　　　The good news is that this is
not a problem. This difficulty is easily
remedied. Once we stop looking to conditioned
mind for clarity, our confusion will fall away.
We sit in meditation not so conditioned mind
will understand, we sit in meditation in
order to see the limits of conditioned mind
and to transcend them.

> ## ONCE WE STOP LOOKING TO CONDITIONED MIND FOR CLARITY, OUR CONFUSION WILL FALL AWAY.

I've sinned too much. Why would meditation help me get to God?

I am endlessly fascinated that we would choose to believe things that are unprovable and that seem to have no purpose other than misery. Who but egocentricity would make such a choice? As long as I believe I am separate from God, that God doesn't want me, I am left with only the support and comfort of egocentricity. Good deal for egocentricity, bad deal for me.

A really helpful question to ask ourselves often as we go down the path of increasing awareness is, "How do you know that?" The little voice appears in the head saying something like, "You've (or I've) sinned too much," and instead of saying

75

"Who says so? How do you know that?" we just roll over and say, "Oh, I guess you're right." Isn't that bizarre!! Someone walks up to you and says, "You have to kill yourself now," and you say, "Oh, okay."
I DON'T THINK SO!!!

So, the first thing sitting still and paying attention might do is get you to question some of these belief systems and ideas that cause you so much misery.

Phones are ringing, kids are screaming, cars are racing by. I don't have a quiet place to meditate. I don't have the privilege of going to a monastery How can I meditate daily?

This is one of the biggest con jobs egocentricity pulls on us. "If my life were different, I'd do all the things I want to do, but it isn't, so I can't." Sometimes I think we've gotten so used to being victims that we've forgotten there are alternatives. Poor me, my life is exactly what I've chosen and now I'm helpless. We're not helpless. And living in a monastery is not an escape from life. The main difference between life in a monastery and life in the world is that in the monastery there are no excuses. Waking up and ending suffering is hard for anybody at any time. The reason it's hard is that we are conditioned to believe our programming of loss and fear and deprivation, not because the circumstances of our lives are difficult. Every moment and every situation is an opportunity either to believe the conditioning and continue suffering or to wake up, see through the conditioning, and end suffering. The _content_ of life is irrelevant. IRRELEVANT.

"But how can people who have no money for food or shelter not suffer?" If it were that simple, most people in the United States would not suffer and most people in places like India and Africa would suffer endlessly. But to our chagrin, we find that we are not happy in spite of our luxury and that often folks we're feeling sorry for are feeling sorry for us.

For each of us, we've just got what we've got, and whatever it is, it's our best opportunity to end suffering if we want to end suffering. As I look at us, it seems that each life is perfect for the person living it. All of the buttons that cause me to go nuts are wired directly into me. I look at someone else who is agonizing over some content or other in life and think, "But that's so easy. Why be so upset over that?" Of course it's easy, it's not MINE. Easy is yours, hard is mine. Simple.

No. It's equally hard and equally easy for each of us. When we're clinging, it's misery; when it falls away, it's peace and joy.

I'm afraid I'll stop breathing when I meditate, and I get afraid to continue

I have a friend who would talk to me about her life with some regularity. She would tell me about something or other that was disturbing her, and we'd explore it together. She would usually start the conversation with "I'm afraid that..." and then would look at career or romance or family or money or whatever. Finally, I grew tired of the endless "whats" and in as gentle a manner as possible suggested that we just explore her fear. The process was fear, the content was endless. In fact, we have a book that addresses exactly that.

I fall asleep when I meditate. Can I play music while I'm meditating?

I suspect that at some point in everyone's meditation career falling asleep becomes an issue. Rather than try to figure out how to avoid that experience, it would be helpful to explore HOW that happens. What is sleep? How does a person fall asleep? How can I be sound asleep during meditation and then wide awake as soon as the bell rings?

Again, what I'm suggesting is not an intellectual pursuit, not an analysis. I am suggesting that you pay such close attention that you can see clearly exactly how sleeping during meditation happens. There is freedom in that.

Will meditation take away my pain?

An old Zen story goes something like this: a student asked a teacher if an awakened person is subject to the law of causation (karma). The teacher answered no. Because of this incorrect answer the teacher was turned into a fox for hundreds of lifetimes. (We don't actually believe this!) Finally the fox encountered a master, explained the problem, and posed the question. The master replied, "The awakened person is one with the law of causation."

Will meditation take away pain? Who can say? For many people their relationship with pain is so different after practice that it would be hard to know if it's been taken away. In a previous question I described my relationship with my injured back. That story addresses this issue in that I couldn't let "getting what I want" be my criterion for happiness. My back was injured, like it or not.

Happiness is the experience we have when we no longer focus on:

Am I getting what I want?

Am I not getting what I want?

Freedom lies in seeing beyond the duality of liking and disliking.

My family thinks I'm doing the work of the devil when I meditate. I have to keep peace with my family, don't I?

If your family decided your youngest child was doing "the work of the devil," would you cease to relate to that child in order to keep peace with your family?

What is peace? Is peace doing what someone else wants you to do regardless of your own experience and direction? If you feel meditation is right for you, but you give it up to keep peace in the family, will you feel peaceful as a result? Will there be true peace in your family? I encourage you to look closely and explore these belief systems.

If one is a Christian, won't meditation take one dangerously away from prayer?

I don't know your definition of prayer, so it's difficult to know what your concern is. For me a sitting practice is quieting. Sitting still enables me to be more focused and present, less distracted. With stillness and presence comes gratitude, openness, willingness, faith, trust, and compassion. I can't imagine any of that interfering with a relationship with Christ.

I might be missing the point of prayer completely, but it seems to me that God <u>knows</u> what I have to say, so it might be most helpful for me to bring to our relationship a willingness to be still, to listen, and to live "thank you."

Do you always have to be sitting still? Is it possible to meditate amidst the activities of daily life?

It is absolutely possible, but most of us are trying to pay attention in the middle of the very circumstances we were taught to be distracted by. So we practice paying attention in the most ideal circumstances we can arrange, thereby attempting to increase our ability to be present at all times.

At a retreat we were talking about practice and one of the retreatants said that as she was growing up she had loved sports practices and piano practice, but she never really enjoyed the competitions or the recitals. When others were watching, she stopped enjoying what she was doing.

The pressure she felt to be better and special ruined the simple pleasure of practicing.

In the same way, we can sit for the sheer joy of sitting and being present, but can then find it difficult to be as present in daily activities with others as we are when just sitting quietly. As we become more skillful at being present, we also become more aware of how much we suffer and are dissatisfied when we are not. This motivates us to find out what the difficulties are and to see through them so that nothing — not conversation, activity, work, discord — can keep us from being fully present to our lives.

Isn't any quiet time as good as meditation? Isn't the point to relax and take "time-out"?

This is one of those "it depends on who you ask" questions, and since you're asking me, I'll answer from the perspective of practice as we do it at our center. No, it isn't. We're not sitting in order to support egocentricity. We're not giving our defenses a rest so that they can hold up against the onslaught of life's pressures. I've talked to many folks who say, "I don't sit. My meditation is running." I say nothing because I haven't been asked, but I feel sad because this is a person who knows and has stopped looking. I just hope they find out that sitting and running are not the same while they still have time and willingness to practice.

Nothing takes the place of stillness and silence in awareness practice. When we stop to consider it, it seems pretty obvious, doesn't it? If you want to be aware on the most subtle level, would you think noise or silence would be most conducive to developing that awareness? Movement or stillness? Notice what you do quite naturally when something happens that you want to attend to closely. You probably stop, say shhhhhhh, and stand very still, attending. You probably don't turn on loud music and start exercising when you want to pay really close attention to something.

Are some types of meditation more intense than others?

I don't know. I suppose that whatever pushes the ego hardest will seem the most intense to that individual. Whatever practice we do it's good to remember that all liking and disliking is ego's domain. If I like intensity and pursue the practice that seems to promise intense experiences, then I am likely to suffer and be dissatisfied with the inevitable times in practice when there does not seem to be much coming up or going on. If I dislike intensity, then I may try to control my practice to avoid strong feelings or intense experiences, and suffer when practice leads in that direction.

If I begin practice because I want to see what causes me to suffer so that

I can have the opportunity to end that suffering, then I will want to learn to recognize the circumstances in which I feel comfortable and secure, and seek out instead those places where I feel threatened, fearful, or inadequate.

As an example, let's say that I want to be a good tennis player. I have a great forehand stroke but a weak backhand stroke. So, of course, I love to hit my forehand and hate to hit my backhand. I try to compensate for my weak backhand by trying to position myself on the court so that I can return with my forehand. I avoid practicing my backhand because it's hard and I hate not being good at it. However, if I am not willing to practice and master that backhand stroke, I will never be a good tennis player because there will always be that weakness in my game, a vulnerable place that my opponents can use to defeat me. I must be willing to practice the part of the game that I am not good at so that I can eventually master it and gain confidence in my ability to handle any situation.

Likewise, in spiritual practice, I want to find those areas where I am not yet skillful so that I can practice and develop the self-acceptance and compassion that will enable me to feel adequate to all of life.

If you're comfortable in your practice it's probably time to go deeper, not as a should, but as a gift to yourself. That which is intolerable to conditioning is often pure delight to our true nature.

How do I justify "navel-gazing" in a world of starving people?

Ah, what a loaded question. Egocentricity would love to write off as nonsense our attempts to examine its control of our lives. So the language is a perfect trap. If we were in fact "navel-gazing," it would be hard to explain in any circumstances. Probably the best explanation would be a simple, "I've never done this before and right now it seems interesting." (Justifying is a whole fascinating topic in its own right. We learned as children that being is not enough. We must do, and we must be able to justify what we do. To whom? Who says so? Good beliefs to scrutinize.)

The fact of the matter is, we are not "navel-gazing." We are scrutinizing in microscopic detail the beliefs, assumptions, and unexammed nonsense that egocentricity uses to control us. Until we realize that seeing through our conditioning is Job One, we will remain confused. My rather rude yet accurate approach to this matter is that the world does not need one more screwed up person trying to fix it. In other words, I don't know who I am; what is motivating me; what the problem is; or what would be truly helpful; but I can't stand the way I feel so I'll go out there and "do something for someone else." Good luck.

A final point about paying attention in a world of starving people: we're talking about awareness and awareness doesn't take time or effort. We can pay attention, we can be aware, while doing anything. It's true that we encourage a period of time each day in which we sit down and face a blank wall in order to practice being aware with as little distraction as possible, but I find it fascinating that we will not hesitate to spend a half hour watching television or reading a magazine or chatting, but it's socially irresponsible to spend a half an hour in silence.

How in the world can breathing and counting bring me closer to God?

I'm sure many would agree that NOT breathing might be the quickest way to getting closer to God, but I don't think that's what you're asking. Who is God? What is God? Are you trying to get closer to God or to your ideas about God? How can being still and quiet take you away from God?

Are meditators peaceful people?

Sometimes, sometimes not. We don't sit to become peaceful, we sit to be present.

Will meditation improve my health, cause me to age more slowly and live longer?

I don't know. You could meditate for many years, assuming you live for many years, and then you would know. Or would you? Conditioned mind wants contests. Conditioned mind wants comparisons and guarantees. None of those things exists except in the illusion of separateness, the world of duality that is the conditioned mind. There is only what is. If you meditate, you will be in whatever state of health you're in, age as you age, and live as long as you live. If you don't meditate, you will be in whatever state of health you're in, age as you age, and live as long as you live. There is no parallel reality in which you are having the opposite experience so you

can make a comparison. That is delusion.
There is only this, only now, only here.

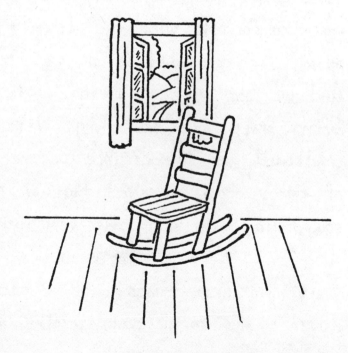

Does sitting get easier over time? I feel like the longer I practice the worse everything gets.

To me those are two very separate questions. Yes, sitting gets easier over time, at least I've never met anyone for whom that isn't true. The body gets more comfortable. If nothing else we get more comfortable with the discomfort of sitting. We get used to it, we accept it. And we get more comfortable with what sitting brings. We see things we're conditioned not to see. We become aware of things about ourselves that we were taught to judge and take very personally.

For a while it seems that every awareness brings another piece of bad news. That's called "going farther and faring worse." The more subtly aware we become the more aware of subtlety we are. As we realize that what we are seeing is our conditioning and not who we are, we can relax and actually learn to be grateful that we're seeing it. Imagine. Because once we know it's not who we are, every insight, every awareness frees us a bit more from the bondage of suffering that is egocentricity.

When I try to relax, I seem to get stiffer and more rigid.

So true. That's because "I" can't relax. Tension is the specialty of "I." Relaxation is the result of accepting what is, of not resisting, of not tensing against anything, including tension.

It seems to me it's easier to sit, to stay present, in a group. Am I imagining this?

Another interesting question! Our thinking and our language quickly lead us down the path of delusion. It is <u>your</u> current experience that it is easier to sit, to stay present in a group. Does that mean it will always be that way? No. Does that mean it is true for everyone? No. Does that mean you should be having another experience? No. All it means is that right now, with your present perspective, this is so for you. It's neither right nor wrong, neither good nor bad. There's nothing to compare it to.

Staying present in a group seems easier for you right now. There is no reason to push this away, no reason to cling to it. And for now, you might consider sitting with a group as much as possible.

I often have insights during meditation. Should I write them down or tell someone or just let them pass and trust they won't be lost?

That's a tough one, isn't it? All this brilliance and clarity—how can I just let it pass through?

Trying to hold on to clarity is like falling in love with a beautiful river and trying to take it home in a bucket. The clarity you are experiencing is the clarity of this moment. Let it go and be present to the clarity of the next moment. Clarity becomes murky pretty quickly when we try to drag it around behind us. If the insight is ever appropriate in another moment, it will be there. Nothing to fear. That's where faith grows.

I know you discourage moving during meditation, but sometimes I feel myself slouching and wonder if it's okay to straighten up when I notice the slouching.

This is where we apply the old Zen saying, "With the ideal comes the actual." We're working so hard, making our best effort to sit up like a Buddha, and somehow, without our noticing, we've become a question mark. Very gently, carefully, mindfully, attentively we straighten ourselves back up with tiny movements that will disturb no one.

As we sit we are constantly auditing our posture, making microscopic adjustments that keep us aligned. This is absolutely within our practice.

I'm sitting in meditation and a mosquito starts buzzing around and then biting. What am I supposed to do?

Pay attention. One of the things I love most about Buddhism, and have from the beginning, is that it is a path of intelligence, not shoulds. All shoulds are based on a belief that we are inherently bad and that left to ourselves we will run amok. Buddhism is based on the knowledge of inherent goodness and a certainty that with the practice of clarity, we will realize our true nature and live from that rather than from our conditioning.

So pay attention. Practice seeing through and past the conditioning that would have you believe that you have to be told what to do because, if not, you'll do the wrong thing. As you practice you will begin to see that you can trust yourself, no matter what. Begin to find out what is so and don't stop, no matter what.

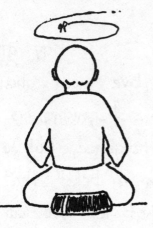

I sit down to meditate and all these feelings come up. It's not peaceful at all so I stop. All I can do is deep breathing.

Are you watching the feelings? Are you staying with them? Are you noticing how you decide you have to stop? Who says so? Do you know how you decided "peace" is the criterion for what is acceptable and unacceptable?

Often at retreats people will ask me how bad a coughing or choking or nausea attack needs to be before they decide to leave the meditation hall. They want to know how to know when they should leave. My response is, "never." It's a bad habit to plan how bad something has to be before we get to quit.

Never. It's never going to get that bad, I'm never going to quit. Will it be hard? scary? unpleasant? Maybe. Could be. Doesn't have to be. (Egocentricity usually decides it's time for us to bail out <u>right</u> <u>before</u> we're going to see something really interesting.)

So the little voice is saying, "You need to get out of here. You're going to do something really upsetting, really embarrassing. You're not going to be able to stand it." And you just sit there. And whatever it is passes, and you live through it, and that little voice of fear and doubt has a whole lot less power over you.

You say there are no shoulds, but everything I read says meditation is a discipline. Don't I need to make myself do it?

A few years ago on retreat a woman came to an appointment with me very excited. She told me that she finally understood self-discipline. I got excited too because I'd never understood it myself, and I asked her to explain it to me. She told me she'd been sitting in the meditation hall when she was just overcome by sleepiness. She remembered hearing me say that it can be helpful to push up with the crown of the head, elongating the spine, when one feels sleepy. She did that and it worked. I said, "That's great. But what does it have to do with self-discipline?" She said she was told to do that, she made herself do it, and it worked. She concluded that making herself do things is self-discipline and that that's what she should do.

I encouraged her to consider another possibility was that she found herself wanting to be awake for sitting, she remembered a suggestion for staying awake, she tried it and it worked. Where's the discipline?

The real discipline is getting past egocentricity in order to let yourself do what you WANT to do. We want to wake up, we want to end suffering, we want to practice being attentive and aware. Egocentricity says, "You can't do that. It's too hard. You don't have what it takes. There's no time for that kind of frivolity. Life is real, life is earnest." All this really means is that if you start an awareness practice, egocentricity might lose control of

your life. So it tries to convince you it's
not right for you.

Let yourself realize you WANT to
practice and then start paying very close
attention to the voices that try to talk
you out of it.

I just can't sit like that for very long. I do much better lying down. Is there anything wrong with lying down to meditate?

There's nothing wrong with anything, but in my experience it doesn't work. If you have trouble sitting upright, practice sitting upright until it's no trouble. Attend to your body, strengthen your muscles. Little by little it will be more comfortable, and not only will you have the joy of a stronger body and easier sittings, you will have taken a little more authority away from the voice who would have you believe you can't.

I was given the technique of counting from one to ten, but I've discovered another way of counting that I like better. Is it okay to change?

Here we have one of the most fundamental issues of spiritual practice. In Buddhism we call this "seeking better accommodation." Egocentricity is in the non-stop, full-tilt pursuit of getting the best deal for itself all the time. Indulging that habit, especially in spiritual practice, is disastrous. The moment you put egocentricity in charge of your practice, you are in deep trouble. We don't practice to make egocentricity happy and comfortable, we practice in order to flush egocentricity out into the light of day so we can see it for what it is.

Keep in mind that we view egocentricity the way we would view a two- or three-year-old child. Is it bad? Is it evil? No, it is simply a single-pointed focus on getting its needs met all the time. The problem is that it is interfering with our lives.

We develop the same relationship with egocentricity that we would with a child: we love it, value you, appreciate it, and take care of it. We do not let it make our decisions, control our moods, sign checks, use credit cards, drive the car...

How do I know when the period is over? Looking at a clock is distracting and I don't like something ticking in my ear. Any suggestions?

You might try putting a kitchen timer somewhere near. They make them now that don't tick. Digital watches that beep can be set to indicate time intervals. An audio cassette can be recorded with a bell at the beginning, one at the end, and silence inbetween.

Be creative.

I could never sit still for thirty minutes. Am I hopeless?

I don't know. The only people I've met who actually seemed hopeless were those who were absolutely invested in believing they were hopeless and in maintaining their hopeless status. It seems that anything is possible, so if a person wants to be hopeless, they probably will be.

One of the things I like best about practice is the realization that whatever one is focused on is one's experience. It is possible to be off in the past or the future, agonizing about something that does not exist in this moment, and suffering mightily. In a split second the attention returns to the breath, to the present, to this moment, and the suffering is gone.

It's exactly like having a sore tooth that only hurts when I stick my tongue in it. When my tongue is not on the tooth, there is no pain. Is it gone? Did it go away? I'd better check. Ouch! It's still there. Take the tongue away, no more pain. Very simple. Likewise, I'm lost in the suffering of conditioned mind, I turn the attention to the breath and no more suffering.

You have no idea what you might be able to do. Look at all the things you've done in your life that you might have thought you couldn't do. We are capable of much more than egocentricity says we are. (It's also a good idea to do much less than egocentricity says we should.) Learn to know what is true for you from center, from your heart, rather than from egocentric conditioning, and you will do and

119

be and experience beyond your wildest dreams. Remember, conditioning limits.

If meditation is a way to end suffering, why should I bother? I don't suffer.

If you know that suffering exists, and if you accept that millions of people experience that suffering in each moment, and if you feel separate from that suffering and those people, you are living in the suffering we are talking about. Identifying with a separate self IS suffering.

This does not mean, however, that you should meditate or follow any other practice designed to end suffering. There is no reason to do or not to do anything. Meditate only if you want to. There are two reasons for this: 1) awareness practice is too difficult to be attempted by someone who is not motivated, and 2) many people begin an awareness practice and find out just how much they ARE suffering. If you are being able to avoid that awareness, why complicate matters?

Meditation is not a contest. It is a path that can lead to compassionate awareness, joy, and peace. From these can grow confidence, prosperity, generosity, gratitude, clarity...

Above all else, if you begin an awareness practice, thank yourself for all the times you do meditate instead of berating yourself for all the times you don't; love yourself for the willingness you have instead of criticizing yourself for resisting; instead of trying to rid yourself of all the things you don't want and cling to the things you do, take a step up and from that greater perspective, embrace it all in compassion.